The New Park

by Ellen Leigh
illustrated by Martin Lemelman

PEARSON

Scott
Foresman

Editorial Offices: Glenview, Illinois • Parsippany, New Jersey • New York, New York
Sales Offices: Needham, Massachusetts • Duluth, Georgia • Glenview, Illinois
Coppell, Texas • Ontario, California • Mesa, Arizona

Mom, Dad, and Norm left their house to take a walk in the neighborhood. They waved to their friends.

"I like our neighborhood," Dad said. "We have a school. We have stores. We have places to eat."

"We can drive our car or ride buses to get around," Mom said.

"We have everything we need here," Dad said.

"We do not have everything we need," Norm said.

"We need a neighborhood park,"
Norm said.

"That is a very good idea," Dad said.
"We can see if other people think so too.
We can have a meeting."

"Why do we need a park?" a neighbor named Ed asked at the meeting.

"We could play sports in a park," Norm said.

"We could sit under trees in a park," Pam said.

"We could take walks in a park,"
Ted said.
   "We could feed ducks in a park,"
Mom said.

"What do you think, Ed? Do you see why we need a park?" Dad asked.

"Yes, I sure do see why we need one," Ed said.

"Let's all help make the park. We can plant patches of grass. We can plant flowers and bushes and trees," Mom said.

Everyone helped. Some people cut
away weeds and thorns. Some people
planted seeds and trees. Some people
made paths. Some people made a place
for sports.

At last the park was done. There were paths. There were benches and trees. There was a place for sports. There was a pond for ducks.

"Now our neighorhood has everything we need!" Norm said.

The One-Room Schoolhouse

Read Together

Communities change over time. Important parts of communities change too. Schools are important parts of communities. Schools are very different today from schools long ago. Most schools today have separate classrooms for different grades. There is a teacher for each class. But in the past some schools were in buildings with only one room. These schools had only one teacher for all the grades. What is your school like?